CHANUK Piano Solos for Kids

Arranged & Edited by
Robert Schultz

PREFACE

Chanukah Piano Solos for Kids includes 11
of the most beloved traditional songs associated with
the celebration of the Feast of Lights. This collection,
as all others within the *Piano Solos for Kids Series*,
is intended to serve as a repertoire and reading supplement
for beginning and early grade piano students.

Teachers, students and parents will find within these pages a body of familiar,
appropriate and reliable music, carefully and expertly crafted into stimulating solo arrangements suitable
for beginners, first-year students and second-year students. The arrangements are written in either a
five-finger format—melodies divided between the hands—or in very simple arrangements for both hands. Fin-
gerings have been included, but sparingly. Tempo indications are in English. Special care has been taken to
ensure that the student will encounter an accurate and consistent approach to editorial marks, providing
a path to a clear understanding and reinforcement of the meaning of these important symbols of the music
language.

Editor: *Robert Schultz*
Project Manager: *Tony Esposito*
Production Coordinator: *Zoby Perez*
Art Design & Illustration: *Jorge Paredes*

CONTENTS

Title	Page No.

AL HANISM 25

BARUCH SHEL CHANUKAH 16

CHANUKAH 6

HANEROT HALALU.................................... 20

I HAVE A LITTLE DREYDL........................... 4

LICHVOD HACHANUKAH 18

Title	Page No.
MAOZ TZUR (Rock Of Ages)	14
MI Y'MALEL (Who Can Retell)	22
MY CANDLES	8
S'VIVON	12
Y'MEY HACHANUKAH	9

I HAVE A LITTLE DREYDL

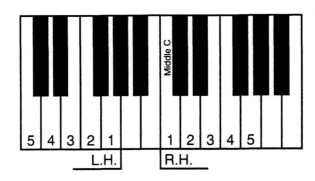

S.E. GOLDFARB
Arranged by ROBERT SCHULTZ

Playfully

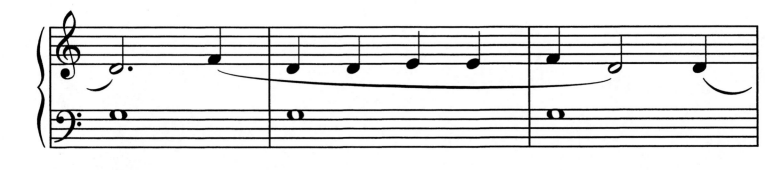

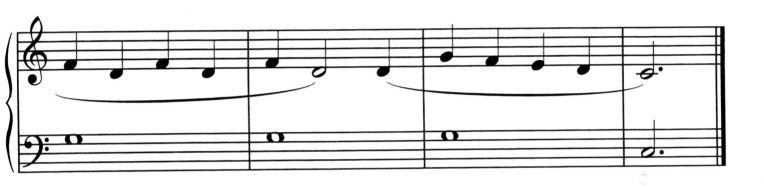

I have a little dreydl,
I made it out of clay
And when it's dry and ready,
Then dreydl I shall play.

Oh, dreydl, dreydl, dreydl,
I made it out of clay;
Oh, dreydl, dreydl, dreydl,
Now dreydl I shall play.

CHANUKAH

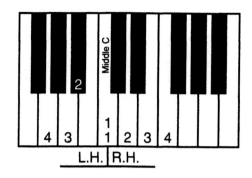

TRADITIONAL
Arranged by ROBERT SCHULTZ

With spirit

Chanukah - 2 - 1
AF9820

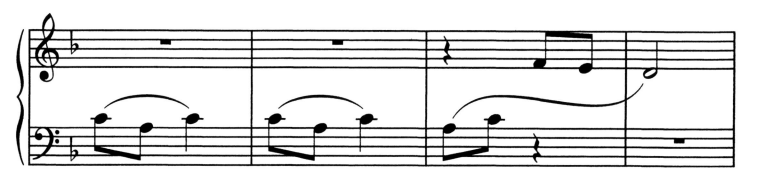

Chanukah Chanukah chag yafe kol kach
Or chaviv misaviv gil l'yeled rach
Chanukah Chanukah s'vivon sov sov
Sov sov sov sov sov sov ma na-im vatov

Chanukah Chanukah, joyous holiday,
Candle light burning bright, helps to celebrate.
Chanukah Chanukah, dreydls spin and turn,
Spin and turn, spin and turn, while the candles burn.

MY CANDLES

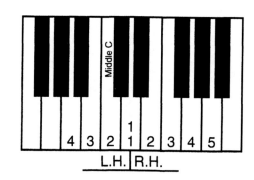

HASSIDIC
Arranged by ROBERT SCHULTZ

In the window where you can send your glow
From my menorah on newly fallen snow,
I will set you, one little candle,
On this the first night of Chanukah.

Y'MEY HACHANUKAH

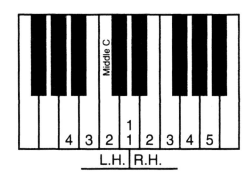

Words by A. EVRONIN
TRADITIONAL FOLK SONG
Arranged by ROBERT SCHULTZ

Moderately

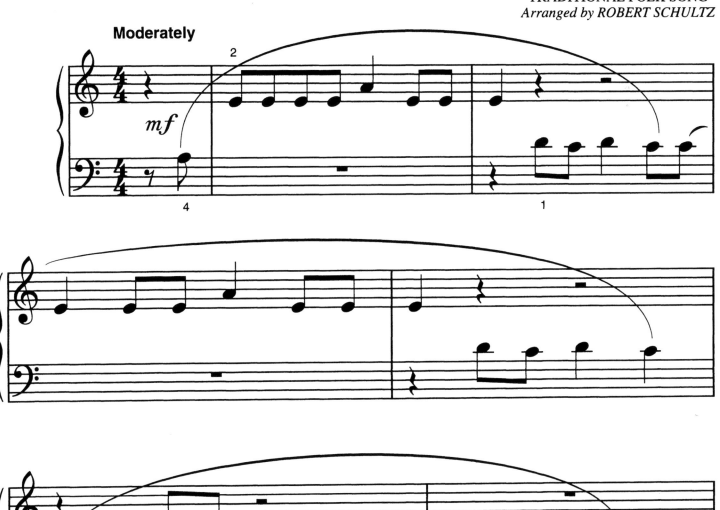

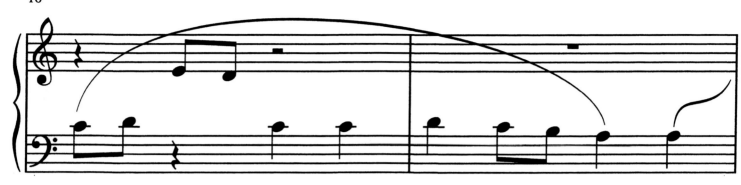

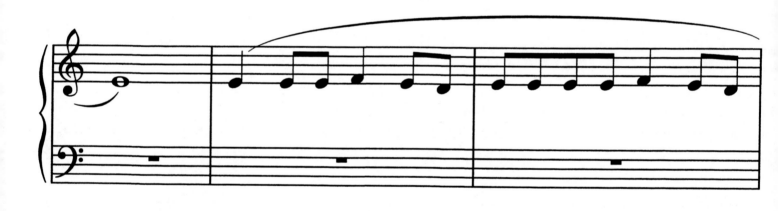

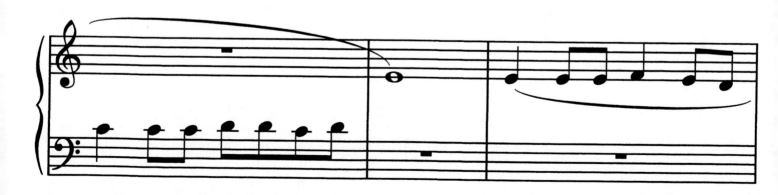

Y'mey hachanukah chanukat mikdasheynu
B'gil uvsimchah m'malim et libeynu
Laila vayom s'vivoneynu yisov
Sufganiyot nochal bam larov
Ha-iru hadliku nerot chanukah rabim
Al hanisim v'al hanifla-ot asher chol-l'lu hamakabim
Al hanisim v'al hanifla-ot asher chol-l'lu hamakabim

Oh Chanukah, oh Chanukah, come light the menorah;
Let's have a party, we ll all dance the horah.
Gather 'round the table, we'll give you a treat;
Dreydls to play with and latkes to eat.
And while we are playing, the candles are burning low;
One for each night, they shed a sweet light to remind us of days long ago;
One for each night, they shed a sweet light to remind us of days long ago.

S'VIVON

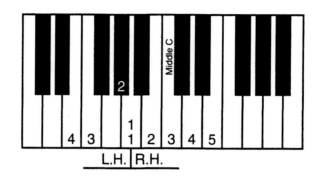

Words by L. KIPNIS
TRADITIONAL FOLK SONG
Arranged by ROBERT SCHULZ

With spirit

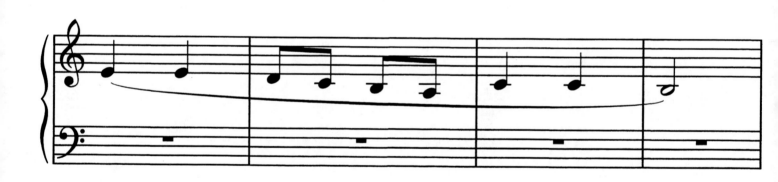

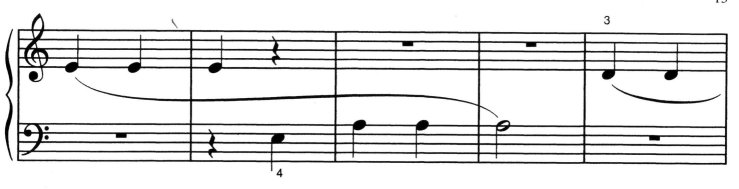

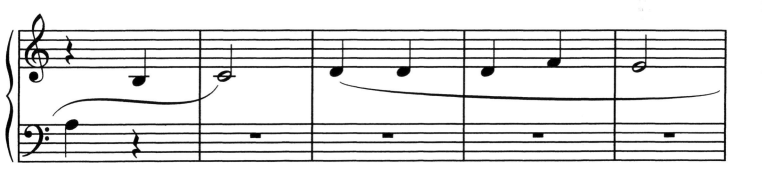

S'vivon sov sov sov	*Little dreydl, spin and turn,*
Chanukah hu chag tov	*On Chanukah when candles burn;*
Chanukah hu chag tov	*On Chanukah when candles burn,*
S'vivon sov sov sov	*Little dreydl, spin and turn.*
Chag simcha hu la-am	*Celebrate with song and prayer,*
Nes gadol haya sham	*A wondrous miracle happened there;*
Nes gadol haya sham	*A wondrous miracle happened there,*
Chag simcha hu la-am	*Celebrate with song and prayer.*

MAOZ TZUR
(Rock of Ages)

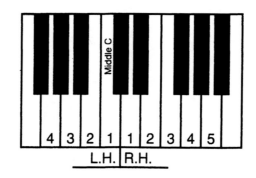

TRADITIONAL
Arranged by ROBERT SCHULTZ

Majestically

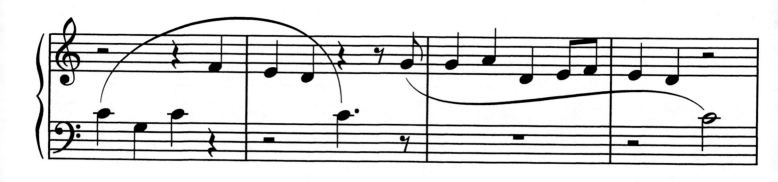

Maoz Tzur - 2 - 1
AF9820

Ma-oz tzur y'shu-ati
L'cha na-e l'shabeyach
Tikon beyt t'filati
V'sham toda n'zabeyach
L'et tachin matbeyach
Mitzor hamn'abeyach
Az egmor b'shir mizmor
Chanukat hamizbeyach
Az egmor b'shir mizmor
Chanukat hamizbeyach

Rock of ages, let our song
Praise Thy saving power;
Thou, amidst the raging foes,
Wast our shelt'ring tower.
Furious, they assailed us,
But Thine arm availed us,
And Thy word broke their sword
When our own strength failed us;
And Thy word broke their sword
When our own strength failed us.

BARUCH SHEL CHANUKAH

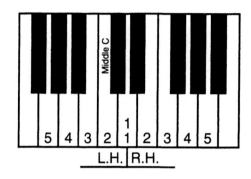

TRADITIONAL
Arranged by ROBERT SCHULTZ

Solemnly

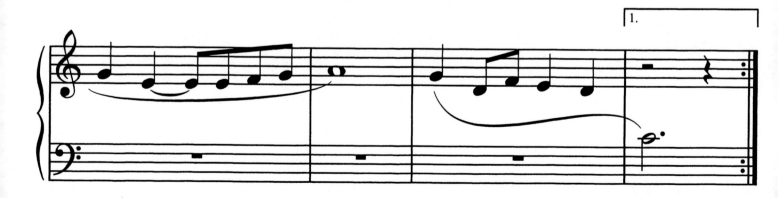

Baruch Shel Chanukah - 2 - 1
AF9820

Baruch atah adonai
Eloheynu melech ha-olam
Asher kidshanu b'mitzvotav
V'tsivanu l'hadlikner
Shel Chanukah

Baruch atah adonai
Eloheynu melech ha-olam
She-asanisim lavoteynu
Bayamim haheym
Baz'man hazeh

Baruch atah adonai
Eloheynu melech ha-olam
Shehechiyanu v'ki-y'manu
V'higi-anu laz'man hazeh

LICHVOD HACHANUKAH

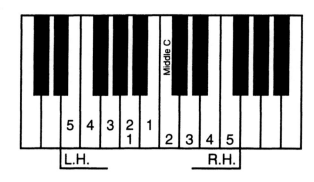

TRADITIONAL FOLK SONG
Arranged by ROBERT SCHULTZ

Moderately

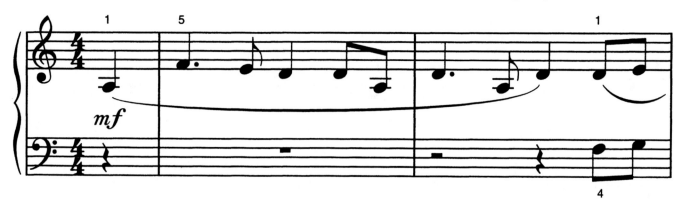

Lichvod Hachanukah - 2 - 1
AF9820

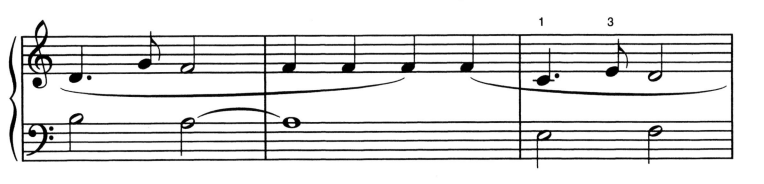

Imi natna levivah li
Levivah chamah umetuka
Levivah chamah umetuka
Yod'im atem lichvod mah
Yod'im atem lichvod mah
Yod'im atem lichvod mah
Lichvod hachanukah

My mother baked me a levivah,
A crisp and brown levivah,
A crisp and brown levivah.
Oh do you know what it's for?
Oh do you know what it's for?
Oh do you know what it's for?
It's in honor on Chanukah.

HANEROT HALALU

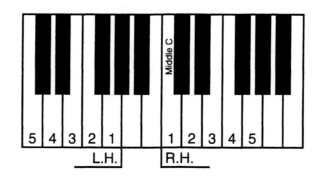

TRADITIONAL FOLK SONG
Arranged by ROBERT SCHULTZ

March tempo

Hanerot Halalu - 2 - 1
AF9820

Hanerot halalu she-anu madlikin
Hanerot halalu she-anu madlikin
Al hanisim v'al hanifla-ot
V'al hatshu-ot v'al hamilchamot

She-asita la-avoteynu
She-asita la-avoteynu
Bayamim hahem bazman hazeh
Bayamim hahem bazman hazeh

MI Y'MALEL
(Who Can Retell)

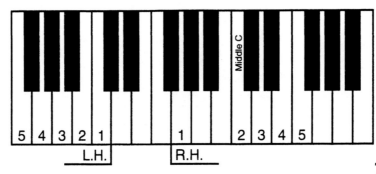

TRADITIONAL ROUND
Arranged by ROBERT SCHULTZ

With spirit

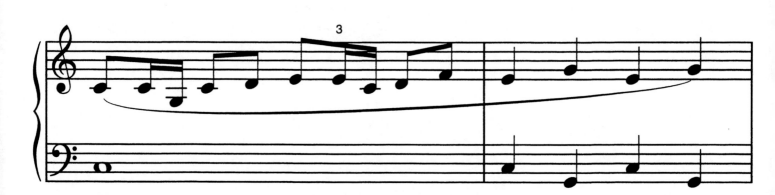

Mi Y'Malel - 3 - 1
AF9820

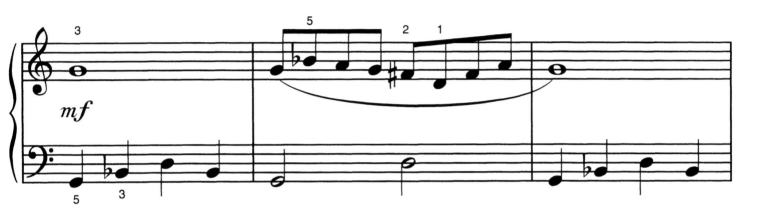

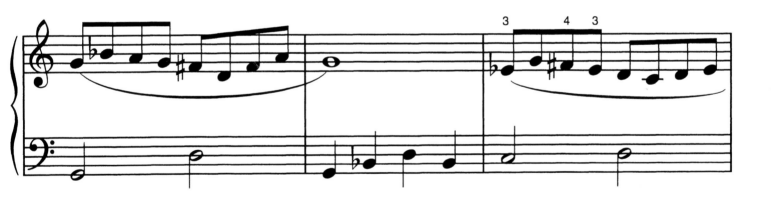

Mi y'malel g'vurot Yisrael otan me yimne
Hen b'chol dor yakum hagibor go-el ha-am
Mi y'malel g'vurot Yisrael otan me yimne
Hen b'chol dor yakum hagibor go-el ha-am

Shma! bayamim hahem baz'man haze
Makabi moshi-a ufode
Uvyameynu kol am Yisrael
Yitached yakum v'iga-el

Mi y'malel g'vurot Yisrael otan me yimne
Hen b'chol dor yakum hagibor go-el ha-am

Who can retell your deeds Israel, those deeds of glory?
Year after year, new heroes appear to make us free.
Who can retell your deeds Israel, those deeds of glory?
Year after year, new heroes appear to make us free.

Hear! Long ago, at just this time of year,
Maccabees arose with sword and spear.
Now our people once more bravely stand,
Building and defending our land.

Who can retell your deeds Israel, those deeds of glory?
Year after year, new heroes appear to make us free.

AL HANISM

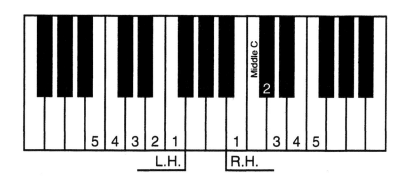

TRADITIONAL FOLK MELODY
Arranged by ROBERT SCHULTZ

Al Hanism - 3 - 1
AF9820

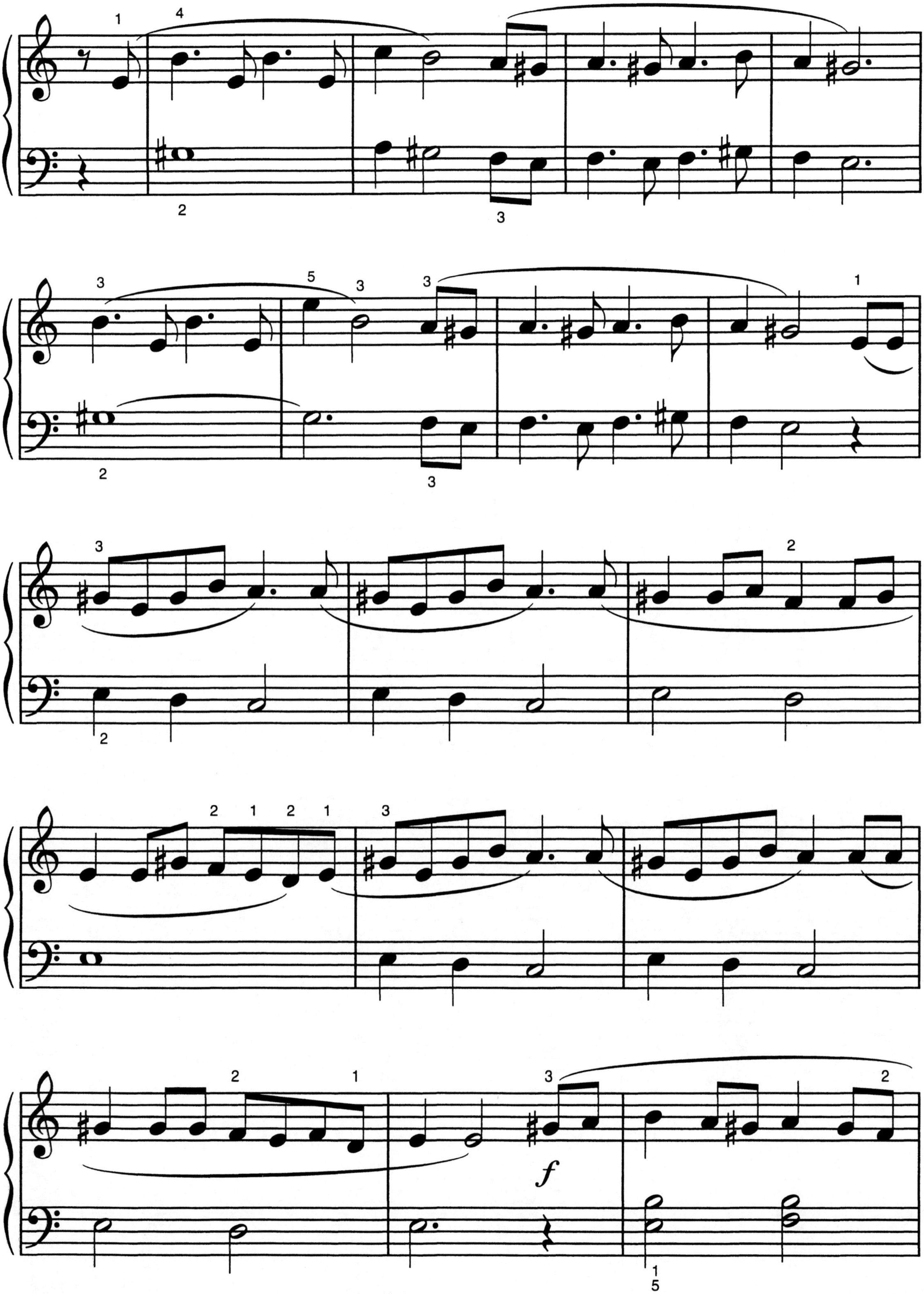
f

D.C. al Fine

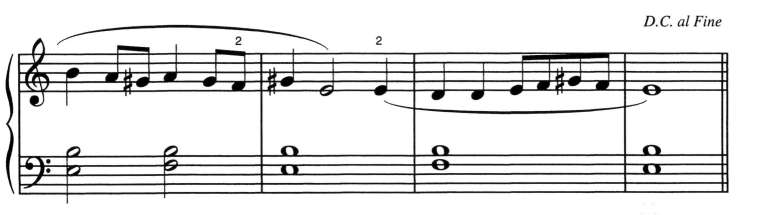

Al hanisim v'al hapurkan
V'al hag'vurot v'al hat'shu-ot
She-asita la-avoteynu
La-avoteynu bayamim hahem
Ba-z'-man ha-zeh

Bimey matityahu matityahu ben yohanan
Kohen gadol hashmona-i uvanav
K'she-amda malhut yavan
Al amcha Yisrael al amcha Yisrael
L'hashkiham toratecha
Ulhaviram mehukey r'tzonecha

V'ata b'rahamecha
B'rahamecha harabim
Amad'ta lahem b'et tzaratam
B'rahamecha harabim